THE FI...
MOTOR R...
IN BRITAIN

BEXHILL-ON-SEA ~ 1902 ~

THE DRIVERS   THE CARS   THE RESULTS   THE PRIZES

taken in part from periodicals of 1902
and in full from the 'Special Motor Races Supplement'
given free with the Saturday 24th May 1902 edition of the
Bexhill-on-Sea Observer
and also from its celebratory issue of 1954

compiled by John Rose

ACKNOWLEDGEMENTS

Autocar, the *Bexhill-on-Sea Observer*, the *Daily Mail*,
Max Le Grand, Brian Hazell and the Bexhill 100,
and Alan Vessey of *Napier Power Heritage*

BOOKMARQUE PUBLISHING

First published May 1997
© John Rose 1977

ISBN 1-870519-40-X

British Library Cataloguing in Publication Data
A catalogue record for this book is available from the British Library

Front cover: Alfred Harmsworth (later Lord Northcliffe) pictured at the wheel of his Mercedes with his wife as passenger outside there Reading home in 1902. The Mercedes was one of Harmsworth's cars taken to Bexhill-on-Sea, stripped of its bodywork and mudguards to partake in the historic Whitsun event, and raced by both Mr Harmsworth and Mr Campbell Muir. Picture courtesy of the *Daily Mail*

Back cover: Leon Serpollet 'racing' along the sea front at Bexhill-on-Sea in May 1902. This actual picture appeared in the 1996 special centenary issue of *Autocar*. Unfortunately *Autocar*'s text in the issue interprets the picture to be of Serpollet at France's 1902 Nice speed trials. *Not so!* The scenery, railway signal and lamp standard are beyond doubt that of Bexhill's sea front.
   Serpollet's passenger is likely to have be Hon. John Scott Montagu M.P., although Mr Roger Wallace did accompany Serpollet on one run. Picture courtesy of *Autocar*

Set in Palatino 11 on 14 pt
Published by Bookmarque
Minster Lovell & New Yatt, Oxfordshire
Printed by Litho Impressions · Oxford. Bound by Cedric Chivers · Bristol

PREFACE

In May 1995 Bexhill-on-Sea was at last officially recognised as the Birthplace of British Motor Racing, and road signs to this effect were erected at the entrances to this small seaside town on the East Sussex coast — obelisks were appropriately placed along the sea front to indicate the start and finish lines of the infamous 'races' which had taken place there in May 1902.

You may ask why it had taken so long to establish this fact? Had it, as some suggest, been swept under the carpet? If so, why? More importantly, why is it that even now, two years after the signs were erected (and mysteriously vandalised on one occasion), this historic event receives scant recognition outside of Bexhill itself? Why do 'authoritative' books like Guinness, the Shell Book of Firsts, the updated *100 Years of Motoring*, the SMMT Centenary Book, and so on, fail to mention it? In the book *Motor Mania* (which accompanied the Channel 4 TV series of the same name) its author claims in the caption to a picture depicting a Napier that had crashed over the edge of a cliff at Bexhill in 1907, that this was: 'clearly the most exciting thing to happen there [Bexhill] for some considerable time...' I beg to differ!

A bone of contention has arisen for some argue that the Bexhill event was no more than 'speed trials' and as such cannot qualify as 'motor racing'. If this little book proves one thing it is that it was both. This was an event previously unparalleled in Britain and it attracted the most notable drivers and cars in Europe, thus qualifying also as the first 'international' racing on these shores.

What can be agreed is it was not 'circuit' racing, but the notion put forward that it cannot be 'motor racing' because it did not take place on a circuit is sheer nonsense.

Of course, the honour of first 'circuit' motor racing in Britain (and the world) can belong only to Brooklands, but Bexhill came very close to stealing that thunder with its proposed 8 mile circuit at Cooden in 1906. Those who entered and partook at Bexhill reads like a 'who's who', they were *the* pioneers and prophets of motoring and motor racing, who may well be turning in their graves at this lack of full recognition for their 'first'.

It was ex-motor racing photographer, Max Le Grand who had stumbled across the background to the May 1902 'races' when he resided at Bexhill-on-Sea in the 1970s. His 2 page feature about the 'races' in *Classic Cars* in July 1976. caused a ripple, but by and large his discovery went unnoticed until his book *Brands to Bexhill* was published in 1995. The first part dwelled on Le Grand's personal life — the Bexhill treasure chest came much later in the book. A couple of reviewers did a hatchet job. One in particular blatantly had not read the book, yet, for reasons best known to himself, resorted to a distasteful and personal attack on Le Grand. All this clouded the Bexhill story. However, TV and especially radio interviews came along. Welsh radio dwelled on the Bexhill discovery; while South-East, Gloucestershire and Oxfordshire radio stations also featured it — the latter county's Fox FM continuing three interviews over as many weeks; then Top Gear's radio slot pitched in with a full interview on the Bexhill topic apparently recorded at the resort itself.

Before I met Le Grand I knew little of the Bexhill event other than a mention by author Chris Mason in his book *The History of British Speed Hill Climbing*. I found from Chris that he had learnt about the Bexhill story from a librarian at the British Library in Boston Spa while he was there researching his book.

The purpose of this little book is to give added weight to this historic 'first' in British motor sport. I believe it contains enough material to rest the case, and hopefully spread the discovery a little further than the south east corner of England.

John Rose, publisher

FOREWORD

Ever since 1907 respected sporting automobilists and historians have revered the Weybridge venue of 'Brooklands' as the "spiritual home of British motor sport". . . and rightly so.

Then a recent discovery provided overwhelming printed and photographic evidence of an event organised in 1902 at Bexhill-on-Sea, East Sussex, that now acknowledges the resort as the official "Birthplace of British Motor Racing".

Prior to 1902 the green shoots of competitive British motor sport had sunk their tentative roots at such make-shift venues as Petersham Hill, Welbeck Park, Colchester and Crystal Palace, where impromptu speed trials were run after the new millennium. The real focus of attention turned to Bexhill where the premier international motor races and speed trials roared into the excited British public awareness.

The Earl De La Warr of Bexhill and his friend John Montagu of Beaulieu, Member of Parliament and a publisher, were wintering on the Côte D'Azur where they became inspired by the Nice Speed Trials taking place along the fashionable Promenade des Anglais. Several members of the Automobile Club of Great Britain and Ireland actually participated.

It was logical therefore that the squire and the club should dovetail their respective ambitions to launch the first motor races in Britain. The Earl readily made available the mettled cycle track that curved along his sea front estate at the east end of Bexhill. The original agreement between the two parties was long standing in the belief that Bexhill would eventually emerge as the British centre of sporting automobilism.

Thus, the first Bexhill Races burst upon the country over the Whitsuntide of May 1902. A crowd estimated at 30,000 celebrated the event which was won by Leon Serpollet driving his own steam propelled car.

Having gleaned impressive media coverage donated to the event by the national newspapers and motoring publications of the time, also keenly augmented by columns of regional and local reportage, it leaves room to wonder why the Bexhill Races have for so long remained the best kept secret at the sharp end of British motor sport history?

This small book will further explain and substantiate Bexhill's rightful claim to be the "Birthplace of British Motor Racing".

Max Le Grand, Cheltenham, May 1997
author: *Brands to Bexhill*

Brands to Bexhill by Max Le Grand.
ISBN 1870519-30-2 hardback 296pp
Copies are available price £19.99 from bookshops
or direct from the publisher.

Unveiling in 1995 of the commemorative stone on the original 1902 Bexhill finish line.

WHIT-MONDAY MOTOR RACES AT BEXHILL.

A WONDERFUL SPECTACLE.

ENORMOUS CROWD OF SPECTATORS

EXCITING RACES.

SERPOLLET'S SENSATIONAL PERFORMANCE.

54 MILES PER HOUR.

SCENES AND INCIDENTS ON THE COURSE.

Reproduced from the Bexhill-on-Sea Observer's 'Special Motor Races Supplement', of Saturday 24th May 1902, the above heading is exactly as it appeared on the front page.

Viewed in every aspect, the motor car race meeting held at Bexhill on Whit-Monday was a great and brilliant success. For weeks the event had been eagerly awaited by motorists and public alike, the latter devouring every fresh announcement with the avidity with which the sporting fraternity follows the preliminaries for a great race, and it speaks much for the character of the whole affair that the highest expectations were more than fulfilled, and everybody satisfied and pleased with the meeting. Spectators were interested and excited, the magnates of the motor world enjoyed their contests and praised the qualities of the track, and the town reaped a good harvest of golden grain, besides securing extensive notices in the English and Continental newspapers. Such a crowd as surrounded the course on Monday afternoon Bexhill has never seen before, and perhaps no event on the South Coast has drawn so many thousands of people together from all parts.

And this Whitsuntide record was established under un-favourable conditions of weather, more suitable for cold and wet October than the middle of the merry month of May.

For four days — Saturday, Sunday, Monday, and Tuesday — Bexhill was given over to the horseless vehicles, which monopolised the streets like they did public interest. No matter

where one might go, he was sure to encounter a car; on the Front and in the principal streets they swarmed in hundreds all the day long, making the place hum with rattling machinery, and causing a cyclonic disturbance of the air as they flew past. If one went into the country roads they were also there, the invasion being so complete and effective that the jobmaster consented to being bearded in his yard, and turned out his horses and carriages to make room for motors of all sorts, shapes, and sizes.

S. F. Edge at the wheel of his Napier leads the procession into Bexhill in May 1902.

Of course, Bexhill has rubbed its hands with delight. Apart from the honour of being the locale of the first automobile races in this country, there was a more substantial satisfaction in the crowd of visitors, who filled up the large hotels and overflowed into every boarding-house which had room to take them, and although Bexhill has always prided itself on its peace and quietness, it apparently has no objection to having its Arcadian stillness disturbed for a time by millionaire motorists and other less wealthy people who drive a car. Truly money can overcome a good deal of prejudice, and in accepting the automobilist with open arms Bexhill is wise in its day and generation.

This picture of a race gives a good distance view of the track and the climb towards Galley Hill with one competitor clearly ahead. However, it is unlikely that this is the 1902 event, rather the 1904.

THE SUNDAY PARADE

A GRAND SPECTACLE

It was a curious, because unusual, sight on Monday morning to walk through the town and see the number of places in which the cars had been stowed away. At every point, and sometimes in totally unexpected quarters one found them "shunting" out into the roadway. The accommodation in Bexhill had evidently been taxed to its utmost capacity. Every person with a clearable building, or shed, or a few feet of open space, would tell you on Sunday of the number of beautiful cars he had on his premises, rolling off a long string of their accomplishments and predictions of what they were going to do on the following day.

At the Bexhill Motor Company's depot in Sackville-road the scene was always animated, and crowds of people gathered to watch the cars as they came up to lubricate. Mr Bradney Williams always had a dozen or so of motors to deal with, but being a smart man of business, and having a large staff of capable men, he was never at a loss to accommodate anybody.

In the mews at the back of the Sackville Hotel dozens of cars had found a shelter, the coach houses being filled with them. Early on Sunday morning the motor "grooms" were hard at work examining the machinery and polishing the shining parts, while other hands removed the pounds of mud which had been accumulated on the journey down. Many people took the opportunity of examining the cars and listening to tales of their achievements from affectionate custodians. One heard, for instance, of a car that had taken part in the French Alcohol race, left Paris at two o'clock on Saturday, came over by the night boat from Dieppe to Newhaven, and motored into Bexhill at nine o'clock. Also of another which came over via Dover, and had scared all the inhabitants en route by its rapid pace, and been challenged by a brave policeman on its arrival in Bexhill because it carried no lights.

The scene on the Bexhill Front on Sunday morning was one of the greatest animation. Thousands of people congregated in expectation of a full dress rehearsal, and they were not disappointed. By eleven o'clock there were scores of cars flying up and down the De La Warr-parade, along the Marina, and in and out of the little streets of the town, as if the drivers had known the place all their lives. Some of the powerful racers appeared later, sweeping by with the rattle of a Maxim, filling the spectators with awe and admiration.

French automobilists, who were in strong force, distinguished themselves by their terrific speed, curves and corners being turned without the application of the brake.

Exclamations of amazement were frequently heard as to the wonderful control exercised over the cars, which seemed more quickly responsive to the steering gear than a horse is to the rein, and it began to dawn on those who had predicted a number of accidents, and busy time for the local undertakers, that when a motor car is driven by an expert the possibility of danger to the public is exceedingly small. The most serious event to be chronicled is the smashing of a terrier dog opposite the Sackville on Sunday morning, the wheels of a car passing over its body; albeit the canine inquisitor was not killed outright, though removed in a damaged condition from the course. At another part of the Front during the day a horse, probably frightened by a passing motor, became restive, and sustained a wound, from which the blood flowed copiously. Apart from these two minor mishaps the prophets of calamity were completely mistaken, and nothing occurred on either of the days to mar the meeting.

The Hon C S Rolls and his Mors.

To the credit of the animal world, it must be said that the horses of Bexhill, probably well accustomed to their strange rivals by now, took very little notice of the whizzing vehicles, and it was noticed that a lady riding mistress did not hesitate to take her charges along the De La Warr-parade when the whole roadway was alive with cars.

Among the most notable motors to be seen out on Sunday was Mr S. F. Edge's famous English-made 75 brake horse-power Napier, which holds the world's records for 1,000 and 100 miles. It is thought to be the heaviest car in existence. Another immense car of ponderous power which attracted attention was the 60 brake-horse power Mors of the Hon. C. S. Rolls. For the benefit of those who do not understand the term "brake-horse power" it may be explained that horse power is a French method of registration, but it is an exceedingly elastic quantity, whereas brake-horse power is a fixed unit of capacity. In this is to be found the explanation of French vehicles of a nominal horse power beating English automobiles of an apparently greater capacity.

Although windy and at times cloudy, the sun shone brightly on Sunday morning, licking up the mud and water from the overnight rain, and giving support to the universal hope that the morrow would be fine.

At noon the first Sunday morning concert took place at the Kursaal, in which the handsome collection of cups and prizes for the races were in view.

The afternoon witnessed a repetition of the morning scenes. The motorists were evidently bent on keeping their cars in good form. Some of them turning from Sea-road negotiated the Kursaal gates with half of a breath of air between the wheels and the piers. A number of the visitors went for a spin in the country, some going as far as Eastbourne. About four o'clock the crowd began to disperse under a heavy cloud, which descended and put a damper on the proceedings for an hour or two, and when the more enthusiastic motors came forth again they found the roads pretty muddy, and the conditions none too pleasant.

The afternoon concert at the Kursaal was largely attended. The

De La Warr Orchestra, 25 strong, discoursed a programme of Wagnerian music under the baton of Mr J. M. Glover, and a recital on the Mustel organ was given by Mr James Coward.

Before Bexhill went to bed preparations for the great event on the morrow were in hand. Seats were placed in the parade gardens, which served as the enclosure, and the course was marked out with tape.

This picture shows the original ornamental gates at the entrance to the track and the Kursaal (theatre/pier). These gates were removed.

SCENES ON WHIT-MONDAY

Monday morning dawned none too promisingly. Clouds of ominous hue were driving across the sky, and at half-past nine a sharp shower came down. The prospects were depressing in the extreme for a holiday crowd, and no more cheerful for the motorists, who could hardly expect to break many records on a heavy track. The pleasure of the meeting was considerably marred by frequent rainfalls during the morning, and at lunch time there was a very heavy shower, which sorely tried the spectators, although they stuck manfully and womanfully to their places, and happily were rewarded by a comparatively fine afternoon. A few trial spins were allowed over the course at seven o'clock, and the small crowd of enthusiasts who were up so early had the delight of seeing Mr S. F. Edge on his 50 h.p. Napier, Mr Jarrott on his 40 h.p. Panhard, which he drove in the Circuit du Nord last week, and Mr Austin on his new 30 h.p. Wolseley.

Before ten o'clock, when the heats of the tourist races started, one had the opportunity of inspecting the arrangements on the course, and the pleasure of finding them in all ways satisfactory. The track, which has been specially reconstructed for motor races, and at great trouble, under the personal supervision of Lord De La Warr and officials of the Automobile Club, was kept admirably clear all day by a large staff of police under the charge of Superintendent Elphinstone, while some members of the Fire Brigade, under Lieut. Wise, also did excellent duty. A few hundred seats, let at 2s. and 1s., had been placed on the south side of the road near the finishing point. These seats, as well as the 5s. enclosure a little farther on, were all occupied during the afternoon, while the roof of the Chalet, commanding a fine view of the course, had a full complement of occupants. A large noticeboard opposite the Hydro, Marine-mansions, denoted the winning post, at which was stationed the judges and timekeepers' tent. The shelter nearest the Kursaal was utilised as a Press box, and in the second, near the grand enclosure, refreshments were dispensed. A private stand had been erected on the east side of the Sackville Hotel. The public also had ample facilities for witnessing the races "free, gratis, and for nothing," the whole length of parade by the side of the track being open to them, besides the spacious slopes of Galley Hill. The occupants of Marine-mansions and other houses on the Front had excellent points of vantage for themselves and their friends, and anybody else who cared to pay a trifling fee for the privilege.

Commencing early in the morning, the stream of people passing by the Kursaal and along the parade gradually increased, until at eleven o'clock there was a deep human border round the entire course of a mile, the crowd in the middle of the afternoon standing in places eight or nine deep all the way to Galley Hill, where thousands watched the starting of the cars, notified to those at the other end by the discharge of a gun. A portion of the roadway from the Sackville Hotel eastwards was utilised as a stand for private motors, carriages, and coaches, giving the scene the aspect of a racecourse without (as the *Daily News* expressed it) the adventitious excitement of gambling. From the balconies and windows of the Sackville fashionably attired ladies and gentlemen of wealth and importance swept the course with their glasses, enjoying a splendid view of the whole track.

In the afternoon the number of spectators could not have been much less than 20,000, although estimates vary from 15,000 to 30,000. The private roadway in front of the hotel served as a paddock, where as many of the racers as space allowed congregated before and after the various contests, to be admired by the owners and drivers' friends and the public. Hundreds of people occupied the bank leading down to the roadway, this being probably one of the best free stands on the course, and at this spot it was a matter of the greatest difficulty to move about. The house next to the hotel on the east, which is not yet let, was full at every window, as was also another building near the Hotel Riposo, by which the Ambulance Brigade patiently waited all day, but fortunately their services were not required.

It was a plucky crowd, undisturbed by wind or rain, and withal good tempered and well-behaved. They had come to see something they had never seen before, and the novelty doubtless pleased them, although they never rose to a state of enthusiasm. Perhaps they felt it would have been like applauding an express train which is out of hearing, and almost out of sight before articulation is possible. But perhaps the real fact which accounted for the absence of any marked demonstrations, and which will have to be altered if the public interest is to be sustained, was the inability of the spectators to follow the races. The programmes were of little use, it was impossible to tell what particular race was taking place until it was over, the huge telegraph board on the Chalet did not always tell the truth, and the events were so inextricably mixed up that if anyone understood them at all it was a few officials, and even they did not appear very clear. The Automobile Club have a lot to learn as to managing a race meeting, and doubtless we shall see an improvement next time, Monday's meeting being the first experience which the Club had had.

The Timekeeper's Chalet with results board.

The first motor racing in Britain

(Above) The motor parade on Sunday and (below) outside the Sackville Hotel.
(inset) Baron Henri de Rothchild's 40 hp Mercedes stripped down for action.
The words 'a racing car' were printed exactly as this in the picture.

The first motor racing in Britain

Crowds begin to gather along the course. Above view looks towards Galley Hill.

Inside the Timekeepers Chalet showing the telegraph equipment.

THE RACES

Racing commenced with the Tourist Section, the motor bicycles being first on the course. The winners in this class romped home so easily that there was nothing to get excited about until the speed trials came on in the afternoon, and then the most immovable were stirred by the sight of throbbing creatures rushing along the track, the driver with bent head and his assistant crouched at his feet to avoid the terrific force of the air. Up go their heads when the winning post is passed, and seeing their rivals behind they cheer with as much breath as they have left, and reduce speed sufficiently to take them through the gates and up Sea-road, whence they pass along Cantelupe-road, and back to the paddock. It was not deemed safe for the heavy cars to race in pairs, so they went over the course singly, and their positions were judged entirely by time.

Naturally the sensation of the afternoon was the flash-like journeys of M. Leon Serpollet on his famous steam cars. In his new steam car, with a wonderful shaped front, not unlike a huge bath turned upside down, the French chauffeur did the kilometre in 41 1/5th secs., representing 54 miles an hour. This was considerably less than his performance at Nice, where he did 75 miles an hour, but in all conscience it was fast enough, and people held their breath in amazement as the car shot by like a cannon ball. Afterwards M. Serpollet went over the course in the "Easter Egg" car, now owned by Mr Creyke, of Oxford, but the time was not so good. The next best time was made by a 20 h.p. Darracq, driven by Baras, who did the distance in 43 secs., equal to 52 miles per hour.

Considering the rain, the track bore the strain very well indeed; even the heavy cars did not cut it up. As the only possible motor course in England, the Automobile Club are to be congratulated on their good luck in securing it, and on his part, Lord De La Warr has again showed his characteristic enterprise and ability to get all the good things at Bexhill. His lordship was most active in promoting the success of the meeting, personally seeing to almost every detail, and he was well backed up by his indefatigable lieutenant, Mr Glover, who was here, there, and everywhere, and his services always at the disposal of everybody requiring direction or information. The cars were able to get a fine flying start down the Galley slope of 160 yards, at the end of which the kilometre of 1,098 yards commences, finishing at the judges' tent, after which there are 260 yards in which to bring the motors to a stop.

Heavy showers interspersed but spirits were not dampened. Brollies at the ready, the huge crowds who lined the course witnessed the first exciting neck and neck motor racing in Britain. Note to the left the purpose built grandstand.

In the class for motor bicycles, weighing not more than 112 lbs. Mr H. Belcher won with a 2 h.p. Humber, driven by Bert Yates, in 1 min. 34/5ths secs. For light voiturettes Mr F. Lewin was first with a 5 h.p. Baby Peugeot of 6^{1}/2 cwt., driven by C. Friswell; time, 1 min. 30^{3}/5th secs.; while in the voiturettes D. M. Weigel was first; time, 1 min. 14 secs. The race for light cars was won by a 12 h.p. Gladiator, weight 13^{1}/2 cwt., driven by G. K. Gregson, in 1 min. 8^{3}/5th secs. The race for cars weighing between 18 and 25 cwt., with seats for four passengers, was won by Mr Mark Mayhew's 20 h.p. Panhard; time, 1 min. 2^{4}/5th secs.; and the race for cars 25 cwt. and over by Mr G. H. Bramson's car, driven by Cecil Edge, in 56^{2}/5th secs. The Pape Cup for the fastest vehicle in the Tourist Class was taken by this car. These were all of the petrol class, and in the race for steam cars first place was secured by Mr J. P. Petty's 6 h.p. Gardner-Serpollet of 19^{1}/2 cwt., driven by A. J. Dew, in 48^{1}/5th secs. The electric prize was won by the car entered by Mr James F. Ochs; time, 1 min. 54^{3}/6th secs.

The motoring pioneer Herbert Austin was often seen at events at the wheel of his Wolseleys. Spectators at Bexhill were privileged with the debut appearance of his new competition 30 hp model.

Two 20 hp light racing cars. On the left Sir James Pender's Darracq driven by French racing driver Gabriel, and on the right Captain Lloyd's similar Darracq (driver Baras).

In the speed trials the Edmunds Cup for the fastest electric racer was won by Mr E. W. Hart's car in the easy time of 1 min. 40^1/5th secs. The first of the motor bicycles was that driven by H. Martin and entered by Mr W. M. Glass, which did the kilometre in 1 min. 1^3/5th secs., Mr Lewis Stroud's 4^1/2 h.p. Soncin being disqualified for being without a proper silencer; and of the racing cycles with more than two wheels the winner was Mr R. Jackson with an 8 h.p. Eagle of 4^1/4 cwt. Mr C. Jarrott's 8 h.p. De Dion was disqualified by the rider pedalling after the first 20 yards. Mr J. S. Overton's car, a 10 h.p. Richard, won the racing voiturette class in 1 min. 17^4/5th secs.

In the class for light racing cars it was a case of Darracq competing with Darracq, and the first place was taken by Mr C. S. Rolls' 20 h.p. car of 12 cwt.; time. 43 secs., equal to 52 miles an hour. Mr S. F. Edge, with a 30 h.p. Gladiator, was first in the special 800 kilogs. (under 16 cwt.) class in 56 secs., but did not take the prize, owing to the minimum of 49 secs. being exceeded.

The 1,000 kilograms class (19 cwt. 2 qrs. 20 lbs.) attracted much interest, as this is the limit weight for racing cars on the Continent. Mr A. Harmsworth's 40 h.p. Mercedes, second in the mile at Nice, was driven over the course by Mr Campbell Muir in 48^3/5th secs.

23

Baron Henri de Rothschild drove his own car, identical with the preceding, in $57^2/5$th secs. Mr Charles Jarrott's 40 h.p. Panhard did the best time, $43^1/5$th secs. The 30 h.p. Wolseley, piloted by Mr Austin, occupied $49^4/5$th secs., while the Hon. C. S. Rolls' 40 h.p. Mors took $44^3/5$th secs.

One of the curiosities of motor engines lies in the fact that in the next class for big racers over 1,000 kilograms, Mr Rolls was driving a 28 h.p. Mors, which develops 60 h.p. on the brake. His

time was 45⁴/₅th secs., beating that of Mr S. F. Edge's 50 h.p. Napier, which shows on the brake 75 h.p. Mr Edge's time was 47 secs., but the course was not long enough for him to use his top speed.

Of other awards may be mentioned the Mark Mayhew 25-Guinea Purse to Mr Jarrott as fastest on the 1,000 kilogramme and special big race classes.

In the final of the light tourist section, newspaper magnate Mr Alfred Harmsworth's 15 hp New Orleans on the left (driven by W. D. Astell) lines up to compete against Mr Clarence Gregson's 12 hp Gladiator. The Lady Pitman £10.10s first prize went to winner Gregson.

"SERPOLLET IS COMING ! "

The Darracqs and the Mercedes cars produced plenty of exciting racing, but the person above all others for whom the crowd was waiting was Serpollet. About five o'clock a white object, identified as his car, could be seen moving about on the top of Galley Hill. Several times there were false alarms. At last the white car was seen to leave with the report of the gun, and the cry: "Serpollet is coming," went through the assembled thousands. They pressed forward for the sensation of the day. The white speck grew larger, and instantly the thing swept by like a meteor, screaming its way through the air, and the telegraph board announced, amid cheers, that the greatest performance of the afternoon had been made, 41 1/5th secs. On completing the course, M. Serpollet was eagerly questioned as to his opinion of the course. "The corners, they are nothing," he replied, "but the road after the hotel" — and he

waved his hands expressively to illustrate its bumpiness — "I have to cut off my fire." Although the kilometre was not covered in the minimum time of 40 secs., it was said that Mr Paris Singer had awarded M. Serpollet the cup in recognition of his sportsmanlike effort.

M. Serpollet is a dark, middle-sized man, with a fringe of black beard. In one short run it was calculated that his car traversed 500 yards at a speed of eighty miles an hour; but M. Serpollet did not like the curves, slight though they seemed, and it was said he had to shut off steam. His second journey in the "Easter Egg" was another exciting fly, but the time occupied was a little longer than the first.

Hon. John Scott Montagu M.P. accompanied M. Serpollet on his steam car and exclaimed that he had never felt the sensation of speed like this car, except when travelling on the footplate of a locomotive!

Among others who took part in the racing or were present were: Mr J. Scott Montagu, M.P., Mr Roger Wallace, K.C., Mr Mark Mayhew, Lieut-Colonel R. E. B. Crompton, Mr Paris Singer, Mr A. F. Bird, Mr J. Ernest Hutton, Mr Henniker Heaton, M.P., Major J. F. Laycock, Mr Campbell Muir, Sir David Salomons, Dr. Boverton Redwood, Mr F. T. Bidlake, Captain S. Smith, D.S.O., Mr W. Crombie and others.

Serpollet tries out his latest car on the Bexhill track.

What the papers said...

A SECOND SAMSON

The *Daily Express* commenced its report with the following:–
"Sunday night found Motorville-on-Sea, as we call Bexhill, quivering with excitement.

Two eminent Frenchmen — M. Serpollet and Baron Henri de Rothschild — inspected the motor course, and found it not to their liking. They objected to the curves; moreover, they held that there was not sufficient room to stop between the finish and the ornamental gates which bear the arms and delight the eyes of Lord De La Warr.

It was a terrible situation. Lord De La Warr offered to carry off the gates in the night, like a second Samson.

However, after a late sitting it was decided that the course was safe enough, if only one of the big racing cars competed at a time. In the smaller classes two cars would have ample room for racing.

It was a pity that such a decision had to be made, for two of the great cars rushing down the track side by side would have been a sight indeed. It is probable that the foreign visitors did not realise that the course, rain-soaked though it was, was of a sort to dry quickly, and that on its gravel there was no chance of the side-slip that makes the muddy plains of France so dangerous to the selected best from the motor stables. As it was, the chauffeurs were decidedly nervous."

PICTURE OF THE SCENE

This is how the special correspondent of the *Daily Telegraph* was impressed by the scene:–

"A broad band with sweeping curves bordered by deep black lines. Half a mile away a white patch appears, drops down the hill at the far end of the course, grows rapidly to the eye into a car, hurtles past like the projectile which its shape suggests, the driver and his assistant crouched low, and is gone like a flash. That is the chief impression left on the mind from the day's motor carnival at Bexhill, and it is the mental photograph of the transit of M. Leon Serpollet's steam car. It is true that its best performance, 41^{1}/5 secs. for the flying kilometre, was only one second ahead of the next best at the meeting — that of the Hon. C. S. Rolls' 20 h.p. Darracq, driven by Baras — and the speed is but fifty-four miles an hour, as compared with seventy-five miles an hour which M. Serpollet achieved at Nice with his previous car. But the impression of pace was much greater, and when he had passed people turned and gazed upon one another with astonishment."

NO BETTER PLACE FOR MOTOR RACING

"Given fine weather," says the *Standard*, "no better place for witnessing motor car racing could be found. The road on one side, and the beach on the other, are at the public service, and yesterday the scene bore no slight resemblance to the run in from Tattenham Corner. On the landward side the rails were lined with motor vehicles of all types. They furnished a realistic idea of the extent to which the industry has grown within the last few years. Many were of an elegant shape, but the tendency still is to follow the old forms of horsed carriages, though in several could be traced the genesis of new designs."

THE "DERBY" DOG

The *Daily News* correspondent noticed an amusing incident:–
"It was a crowd of sportsmen and sportswomen, and when the rain came down they held their ground without flinching. The similarity to the racecourse was carried out even to the appearance of the "Derby" dog, who would persist in trotting down the course just as some car was sent upon its way. As Stephenson remarked of the cow, it would have been bad for the dog, but fortunately the canine wanderer was hustled off the track before he could immolate himself before the Juggernaut of automobilism."

Tourist Voiturette class – 8 hp New Orleans (on the left) against a 12 hp Gladiator.

OFFICIALS

The following were the officials:–

Ex-officio Officials: Mr Roger W. Wallace, K.C. (*chairman of the Club Committee*), Hon. John Scott Montagu, M.P. (*vice-chairman*), Mr Mark Mayhew, L.C.C., (*vice-chairman*), Lieut.-Colonel R. E. B. Crompton, C.B. (*vice-chairman*), and Mr Paris Singer (*hon. treasurer*).

Races Committee: Mr Mark Mayhew, L.C.C. (*chairman of the Races Committee*), Mr Alfred F. Bird (*vice-chairman of the Races Committee*), Mr Rupert E. Beckett, Mr S. F. Edge, Mr J. Ernest Hutton, Mr C. Jarrott, Major J. F. Laycock, D.S.O., the Hon. John Scott Montagu, M.P., Mr Campbell Muir, Hon. C. S. Rolls, Sir David Salomons, Bart. and Mr Roger W. Wallace, K.C.

The Club Secretary: Mr C. Johnson.

Hon. Marshals of the Course: Mr Mark Mayhew, L.C.C. (*chairman of the Races Committee*), and the Right Hon. the Earl De La Warr.

Hon. Judges: Mr Alfred F. Bird and Dr. Boverton Redwood.

Referee for Time Records: Lieut-Colonel R. E. B. Crompton, C.B.

Hon. Starters: Mr Edward Monville and Mr R. B. B. Bruce.

Hon. Timekeepers: Mr Robert E. Phillips (who took the time by his electric timing apparatus), Mr Harry J. Swindley (*Hon. official timekeeper to the A.C.G.B.I.*), Mr F. T. Ridlake, and Mr E. R. Shipton.

Hon. Assistant Timekeeper at the start: Mr Rees Jeffries.

Extra Timekeeper: Mr T. D. Dutton.

DETAILS OF THE RACES

TOURIST SECTION

THE "PAPE" 25-GUINEA CUP, presented by Mr E. J. Pape, of Moor Hall, Bexhill, awarded to the fastest car (not cycle) over the course in the Tourist Section without a reference to class. The winner in each class (except cycles) competed for this Cup. Steam cars were excluded from competition. This Cup to be run for at the end of the events in the Tourist Section.

CLASS F II — Motor Bicycles weighing not more than 112 lbs. Entrance fee, half-a-guinea. Heats of four. Prizes: Silver Medal for the winner, and bronze medal for the second.

The racing started with the motor bicycles, weighing not more than 112 lbs., at five past ten o'clock.

Mr E. H. Arnott's 2 h.p. Werner beat Dr. Whitehall Cooke's 1¾ h.p. Phoenix.

Mr H. L. Belcher's 2 h.p. Humber beat an unnumbered cycle.

There were nine entries for this, the winner in the final being Mr H. Belcher, with his 2 h.p. Humber (time 1 min. 3 ⁴/5th secs.), driven by Bert Yates; second, Mr E. H. Arnott's 2 h.p. Werner, driven by himself.

CLASS F I — Motor cycles having more than two wheels and weighing not more than 2 cwt. Entrance fee, half-a-guinea. Heats of four. Prizes: Silver medal for the winner, bronze medal for the second. Mr W. J. Crompton, with his 4½ h.p. Soncin, entered, but was ruled out for over weight.

CLASS E — LIGHT VOITURETTES — Cars weighing less than 10 cwt., with seats for four persons. Cars weighing less than 9 cwt., with seats for three persons. Cars weighing less than 8 cwt., with seats for two persons. Entrance fee, one guinea. Heats of two. First prize, prize given by Messrs. W. Bishop and Co., 88, George-street, Croydon; second prize, prize value £7, given by Messrs. G. Skudder and Co., 98, Tooley-street, London, S E.

Mr F. Lewin's 5 h.p. (Baby) Peugeot beat Mr J. H. Gorham's 4½ h.p. De Dion and Mr G. D. Barnes' 6 h.p. M.M.C.

Mr Ralph Jackson's 8 h.p. Eagle Tandem beat Mr R. W. Leader's 6½ h.p. Century Tandem.

Mr E. W. Hart's 16 h.p. British Electromobile Co., beat Mr R. W. Wallace, K.C.'s, Krieger in 1 min. 40½ secs.

There were seven entries for this. In the final the winner was Mr F. Lewin, with his 5 h.p. (Baby) Peugeot (time, 1 min. 30 ³/5th secs.), driver C. Friswell. Mr G. D. Barnes' 6 h.p. M.M.C. was second, driven by himself.

CLASS D — VOITURETTES — Cars weighing less than 15 cwt., with seats for four persons. Cars weighing less than 13½ cwt., with seats for three persons. Cars weighing less than 12 cwt., with seats for two persons. Entrance fee, one and a half guineas. In heats of two. First prize, prize value fourteen guineas, given by Mr Charles Bardies, 54, Long Acre, London; second prize, prize value £9, given by Messrs. G. Skudder and Co., 98, Tooley-street, London, S.E.

Mr W. H. Astell's 8 h.p. New Orleans beat Mr Geo. H. Kahn's 7 h.p. Panhard.

Mr J. Overton's 10 h.p. Richard beat Mr W. J. Crampton's 10 h.p. Decauville.

Mr S. F. Edge's 12 h.p. Gladiator beat Mr W. H. Astell's 8 h.p. New Orleans. A good race, the winner passing the post a few feet ahead.

Mr H. Smith's 8 h.p. De Dion beat Mr J. Overton's 10 h.p. Richard.

There were eleven entries, the winner in the final being Mr Herbert Smith, with his 8 h.p. Clement, transferred from Class B, Speed Section (time, 1 min. 14 secs.), driver, D. M. Weigel. Mr E. de Wilton's 8 h.p. De Dion was second, driven by himself.

Class C. Mr R. L. Elliott's 14 hp Déchamps (on the left) against Mr J. E. Hutton's 15 hp Mors.

CLASS C — LIGHT CARS —Cars weighing less than 18 cwt., with

seats for four passengers. Cars weighing less than 16 cwt., with seats for three persons. Cars weighing less than 14 cwt., with seats for two persons. Entrance fee, two guineas. In heats of two. First prize, the Lady Pitman £10 10s. prize, presented by Lady Pitman, of Penn-hill, Weston, Bath; second prize, prize value five guineas, given by Messrs. Alfred Russell and Co., Bedford Works, Walsall.

Mr Charles Jarrott's 7 h.p. Panhard beat Mr Mark Mayhew's 7 h.p. Panhard.

Mr H. Hewetson's 7 h.p. Benz beat Dr. Doverton Redwood's 7 h.p. Panhard.

Mr Roger H. Fuller's 10 h.p. Panhard beat Mr H. Hewetson's 9 h.p. Benz.

Mr Clarence Gregson's 12 h.p. Gladiator beat Mr H. Belcher's 12 h.p. Humber.

Mr J. S. Critchley's 12 h.p. Brush beat Mr George Iden's 10 h.p. M.M.C.

Mr H. Austin's 10 h.p. Wolseley beat Mr Ross Browne's 10 h.p. Panhard.

Mr J. A. Holder's 10 h.p. Lanchester beat Mr H. Hewetson's 7 h.p. Benz.

Mr Roland Browne's 10 h.p. Lanchester beat Mr M. H. Bucklea's 10 h.p. M.M.C.

Mr J. E. Hutton's 15 h.p. Mors beat Mr R. L. Elliott's 14 h.p. Déchamps.

Mr Roger H. Fuller's 10 h.p. Panhard beat Mr H. Hewetson's 7 h.p. Benz.

Mr Clarence Gregson's 12 h.p. Gladiator beat Mr J. S. Critchley's 12 h.p. British.

Mr A. C. Harmsworth's 14 h.p. New Orleans beat Mr Chas. Jarrott's 7 h.p. Panhard.

Mr J. E. Hutton's 15 h.p. Mors beat Mr Roland Browne's 10 h.p. Lanchester.

Mr Clarence Gregson's 12 h.p. Gladiator beat Mr Roger H. Fuller's 10 h.p. Panhard.

Mr A. C. Harmsworth's 14 h.p. New Orleans beat Mr J. E. Hutton's 15 h.p. Mors.

Mr Clarence Gregson's 12 h.p. Gladiator beat Mr H. Austin's 10 h.p. Wolseley.

There were 19 entries. In the final Mr Clarence Gregson's 12 h.p. Gladiator (driver, C. K. Gregson) won (time, 1 min. 8 3/5th secs.), the second being Mr Alfred C. Harmsworth's 14 h.p. New Orleans, driver, W. D. Astell.

CLASS B — 18 cwt. AND OVER — Cars weighing 18 cwt. or more, but less than 25 cwt., with seats for four passengers. Entrance fee, two and a half guineas. In heats of two. First prize, prize value twelve guineas, given by Messrs. Salsbury and Son, Ltd., Green-street, Blackfriars, London, S. E.; second prize, prize value £4 10s., presented by Messrs. A. W. Gamage, Ltd., Holborn, London.

Sir James Pender's 20 h.p. Darracq beat M. Godard Desmarest's 20 h.p. Darracq.

Mr A. G. Schiff's 12 h.p. Panhard beat Mr C. Cordingley's 12 h.p. M.M.C.

There were twelve entries. In the final Mr Mark Mayhew won with his 20 h.p. Panhard (time, 1 min. 2 4/5th secs.). The second was Mr A. G. Schiff's 12 h.p. Panhard (driver, Yves Le Coadon).

CLASS A — 25 cwt. AND OVER — Cars weighing 25 cwt. or more, with seats for four passengers. Entrance fee, two and a half guineas. In heats of two. First prize, Mr Charles Cordingley's 25-Guinea Cup; second prize, prize value £12 12s., given by the United Motor Industries, Ltd., 42, Great Castle-street, Oxford-street, London, W.; third prize, prize value £10, given by Messrs. G. Skudder and Co., 98, Tooley-street, London, S. E.

Mr W. G. H. Bramson's 50 h.p. Napier beat Mr H. T. Edwards' 24 h.p. Mors (Cecil Edge being the driver of the winning car) in 59 1/2 secs.

Mr W. G. H. Bramson's 50 h.p. Napier beat Mr Edwin Midgley's 16 h.p. Napier.

Mr Walter Crombre's 16 h.p. Daimler beat Mr Harvey de Cros' 16 h.p. Panhard and Mr L. Savory's 2 1/4 h.p. Orient.

Mr Edwin Midgley's 16 h.p. Napier beat the Hon. John Scott Montagu, M.P.'s, 24 h.p. Daimler.

Mr Edwin Midgley's 16 h.p. Napier beat Mr Walter Crombre's 16 h.p. Daimler.

There were eight entries, the winner in the final being Mr W. G. H. Bramson, with his 50 h.p. Napier (time, 56^2/5th secs.), driven by Cecil Edge. The second was Mr Edwin Midgley's 16 h.p. Napier driven by himself.

The "Pape" Cup for the fastest car over the course in the Tourist Class, Winners in each Class (except cycles and steam vehicles) eligible. In heats of two. Was won by Mr Bramson's 50 h.p. Napier.

RACE FOR TOURIST STEAM VEHICLES — Entrance fee, one and a half guineas. In heats of two. Prizes: First prize, prize value £6 15s., given by the United Motor Industries, 42, Great Castle-street, Oxford-street, London, W. Bronze medal for the second.

Mr J. P. Petty's 6 h.p. Gardner-Serpollet to the left and Mr W. Letts' 5^1/2 h.p. Locomobile.

Mr J. P. Petty's 6 h.p. Gardner-Serpollet beat Mr J. W. H. Dew's 10 h.p. Gardner-Serpollet.

Mr W. Letts' 5^1/2 h.p. Locomobile beat Mr R. Laurence's 10 h.p. Miesse.

Mr W. Letts' 5$1/2$ h.p. Locomobile beat Mr A. T. Salsbury Jones' 6 h.p. Miesse.

There were six entries. In the final Mr J. P. Petty's 6 h.p. Gardner-Serpollet, driven by A. J. Dew, was victorious (time, 48$1/5$th secs.), the second being Mr W. Letts' 5$1/2$ h.p. Locomobile, driven by himself.

RACE FOR ELECTRIC TOURIST VEHICLES — Entrance fee, one and a half guineas. In heats of two. Prizes: First prize, prize value £5 5s., given by Messrs. S. Smith and Son, 9, Strand, London, W. C.; bronze medal for the second.

There were three entries, the winner being Mr James F. Ochs, with his City and Suburban (time, 1 min. 54$3/5$th secs.). Mr Theodore G. Chambers' B. Electromobile Co. was second.

SPEED SECTION

CLASS E — ELECTRIC RACING VEHICLES. Entrance fee, three guineas. In heats of two. Prize, the fastest car to receive the "Edmunds Cup," presented by Mr Henry Edmunds, member of the Committee of the Automobile Club of Great Britain and Ireland.

There were two entries, Mr E. W. Hart's 16 h.p. B. Electromobile Co. (driver, Jeal) being first (time, 1 min. 40 $1/5$th secs.), and the Krieger, of Mr Roger W. Wallace, K.C., being second; driven by himself.

CLASS D — MOTOR BICYCLES WEIGHING OVER 112 lbs. Entrance fee, half a guinea. In heats of four. Prizes: The winner receives the *Motor Cycling* Cup, presented by the proprietors of *Motor Cycling*, provided that, if there are not two starters, the winner covers the flying kilometre in 63 $4/5$th secs. — 35 miles per hour. Second will receive a silver medal.

Mr William Glass's 2 $3/4$ h.p. Excelsior beat Mr S. F. Edge's 2$1/2$ h.p. Chapelle.

Mr Lewis Stroud's 4 h.p. Soncin beat Mr E. Blount's 2$3/4$ h.p. Shaw.

There were nine entries, the winner in the final being Mr William Glass, with his 2 3/4 h.p. Excelsior, driven by H. Martin (time, 1 min. 1 3/5th secs.). Mr E. Blount's 2 3/4 h.p. Shaw was second (driver, S. A. East). Mr Lewis Stroud's 4 1/2 h.p. Soncin was entered; but he was disqualified for riding without a proper silencer.

CLASS D1 — RACING MOTOR CYCLES having more than two wheels, and weighing over two cwt., but under 250 kilos — 4 cwt. 3 qrs. 20 lbs. Entrance fee, half-a-guinea. In heats of four. Prizes: The winner will receive the prize, value £6 6s., given by Messrs. Boyd and Co., 296, Regent-street, London, W., provided that, if there are not two starters, the winner covers the flying kilometre in not more than 55 secs – 40 miles per hour. The second receives a silver medal.

There were four entries, Mr Ralph Jackson winning with his 8 h.p. Eagle, driven by himself. Mr Charles Jarrott, who entered his 8 h.p. De Dion, was disqualified for pedalling after the 20 yards' limit.

Mr J. S. Overton's 10 hp Georges Richard (right) about to defeat Mr T. B. Browne's 9 hp Novelty.

CLASS C — RACING VOITURETTES — Vehicles under 400 kilogs. (7 cwt. 3 qrs. 14 lbs). Entrance fee, two guineas. Over the whole course, Driver only, no second passenger. In heats of two. Prizes: The winning car to receive the "De La Warr" 30 Guinea Cup, presented by Earl De La Warr, provided that, if there are not two starters, the winner covers the kilometre in not more than 55 secs. — 40 miles per hour. The second to receive a silver medal.

There were three entries. The winner in the final was Mr J. S. Overton, with his 10 h.p. Richard (time, 1 min. 17⁴/5th secs.), the second being Mr T. B. Browne's 9 h.p. James and Browne, driven by himself.

CLASS B — LIGHT RACING CARS — Vehicles under 650 kilogs. (12 cwt. 3 qrs. 5 lbs.). Entrance fee, three guineas. In heats of two. Prizes: The fastest car to receive the *Country Gentleman* 25-Guinea Cup, presented by the proprietor of *The Country Gentleman*, provided that if there be not two starters the winner covers the flying kilometre in not more than 49 secs. — 45 miles per hour.

The Hon. C. S. Rolls' 24 h.p. Mors beat Mr A. G. Schiff's 12 h.p. Panhard.

There were four entries. The Hon. C. S. Rolls' 20 h.p. Darracq (driver, Baras), was first (time, 43 secs.). Sir James Pender's 20 h.p. Darracq (driver, Gabriel) was second.

The above reference to C. S. Rolls' Darracq (*Bexhill-on-Sea Observer*) is incorrect, according to *The Car* magazine Baras drove Captain Lloyd's Darracq. See also on p.23.

CLASS S — SPECIAL 800 KILOGS. CLASS — Vehicles weighing more than 650, but less than 800 kilogs. (15 cwt. 2 qrs. 27 lbs.). Entrance fee, three guineas. In heats of two. Prizes: The fastest car to receive the "Holder" Ten Guinea Prize, presented by Mr J. A. Holder, of Pitmaston, Moor Green, Birmingham, provided that the winner covers the flying kilometre in not more than 49 secs. — 45 miles per hour.

There were four entries. Mr S. F. Edge, with his 30 h.p. Gladiator (driver, Mercier) won the final in 56 secs., but did not take the prize, as the time was beyond the limit.

There were 10 entries for 'The Car' Cup. Baron Henri de Rothschild was one — he came 5th in his 40 hp Mercedes, well behind the winner, Charles Jarrott. The entry list also included renowned French racing drivers Léonce Girardot and Réné de Knyff, but neither put in an appearance.

CLASS A — 1,000 KILOGS. RACERS — Vehicles under 1,000 kilogs. (19 cwt. 2 qrs. 20 lbs.). Entrance fee, four guineas. In heats of two. Prize: The owner of the fastest car to receive the 25-Guinea *Car Illustrated* Cup, presented by the proprietors of *The Car Illustrated*, subject to the kilometre being covered in not more than 40 secs. — 55 miles per hour.

There were ten entries, the final results being:–

1, Mr Charles Jarrott's 40 h.p. Panhard, driven by himself (time, 43^1/5th secs.); 2, the Hon. C. S. Rolls' 40 h.p. Mors driven by himself (time, 44^3/5th secs.); 3, Mr Alfred C. Harmsworth's 40 Cannstatt Daimler Mercedes (driven by Campbell Muir, time, 48^3/5th secs.); 4, Mr H. Austin's 30 h.p. Wolseley (time, 49^4/5th secs.); 5, Baron Henri de Rothschild's 40 h.p.Cannstatt Daimler Mercedes, driven by himself (time, 57^2/5th secs.).

Mr Alfred Harmsworth's 40 hp Mercedes, stripped for racing, took 3rd place in The Car Cup *race. The driver was Mr Campbell Muir.*

Winner of 'The Car' Cup, Charles Jarrott (right) at the wheel of his 40 hp Panhard. Pictured alongside is the Hon. C. S. Rolls who came second on his 40 hp Mors.

SPECIAL BIG RACERS' CLASS — Vehicles over 1,000 kilogs. (19 cwt. 2 qrs. 20 lbs.). Entrance fee, five guineas. Prize: The fastest car to receive the *Daily Express* 50-Guinea Cup, presented by the *Daily Express*, provided that, if there are not two starters, the flying kilometre is covered by the winner in not more than 40 secs. — 55 miles per hour. The second to receive a silver medal.

Mr S. F. Edge's 50 h.p. Napier, driven by himself, accomplished the distance in 47 secs., the Hon. C. S. Rolls' 28 h.p. Mors, driven by himself, being first, with 45 4/5th secs. These were the only entries.

RACING STEAM CARS — Entrance fee, three guineas. In heats of two. The winner (or, if the winner becomes holder of the *Daily Mail* Cup, the second) to receive the "Paris Singer" 25-Guinea Cup, presented by Mr Paris Singer, Honorary Treasurer of the Automobile Club of Great Britain and Ireland, provided that if

'The Car' *Cup*

there are not two starters, the flying kilometre is covered by the winner in not less than 40 secs. — 55 miles per hour. The second to receive a silver medal.

For this important competition there were three entries, the result being: — 1, Mons. L. Serpollet, with his Gardner-Serpollet, Paris, driven by himself (time, 41¹/₅th secs.); 2, Mr Clement Peache's 6 h.p. Gardner-Serpollet (driver, L Perry-Keen; time, 57³/₅th secs.); 3, Mr Arthur Clay's Locomobile Co. of America (driver, A. Ginder; time, 1 min. 18⁴/₅th secs.).

Mons. Serpollet's effort was the best time for the day, being at the rate of 54.55 miles an hour. Owing to the upsetting of an oil bottle flames burst out upon Mons. Serpollet's car just as he covered the course. He leaped down and beat out the threatened conflagration, and springing back again, proceeded on his way, going over the course again; but his time was 43 secs. In view, however, of his sportsmanlike attempt, the donors have decided to present him with the Cup, although the minimum speed was not reached.

The "Mark Mayhew" 25-Guinea Purse, presented by Mr Mark Mayhew, L.C.C., vice-chairman of the Automobile Club, and chairman of its Races Committee. The Purse to be given with a Club medal to the faster in a competition over the full course (or over a flying kilometre, as may be hereafter directed) of the cars which win respectively in Class A of the Speed Section and the Special and the Special Class for Big Racers.

This was won by Mr Charles Jarrott; time, 43^1/5th secs.

Crowds gather round Serpollet's car after it catches fire, caused by a upturned oil bottle. Serpollet is said to have leapt from his car and beat out the flames himself, then carried on amid hearty cheers.

Mr Arthur Clay's American Locomobile driven by A. Ginder.
Note the wind cheating device fitted.

THE BEAUTY COMPETITION
PEALL WINS THE BEXHILL CUP

When the course was free from racing motors, the last speed trial being over, forty cars in full dress swept on the track past the Sackville Hotel, and slowly made their way past the grand enclosure. This was the competition for the car having the best appearance, or the best looking turnout, a stringent condition being that the vehicle should not be decorated with flowers or ribbons. The procession was a most imposing and interesting display of some of the best work of the makers, cars of every type, colour, and size, coming forth in a spic and span condition, with burnished metal and shining paint, veritable things of beauty, exciting the admiration of all beholders. Several times were the cars driven before the judging Committee, who had no little difficulty in arriving at a just decision, so equally strong were the claims of many of the vehicles. On one large car the attendant sat behind in uniform, like a footman. The prizes being the House of Commons 40-Guinea Cup and the Bexhill-on-Sea "Welcome" Cup, the judges were selected from the Lower House of Parliament and residents of Bexhill, the appointed representatives of the former being Mr J. Scott Montagu, Mr Thomas Dewar, and Mr Charles Shaw, while the following also participated in the choice: — Earl De La Warr, Lady Mary Sackville, Colonel Newnham Davis, Miss Dora Pape, Mrs Bathurst, Mrs Cohen, Mrs Peachey, and Mrs Manning. The points taken into consideration were elegance of design, finish and appointments, comfort, and smartness, combined with suitability of dress of occupants. The premier award went to Mr S. F. Edge for his 16 h.p. Napier, containing four seats. The Bexhill Cup was won by Mr W. J. Peall, the celebrated billiard player, who sat in a handsome 12 h.p. Daimler. The third prize, a banner presented by the Automobile Club, went to Mr Astell, for his 8 h.p. New Orleans.

Subsequent to this the cups and prizes were presented in the enclosure by Lady Mary Sackville, who performed the function very gracefully. Lady Mary was heartily thanked for her kindness, cheers being given for her and Lord De La Warr.

This practically brought the long day's sport to a close, so far as open-air events were concerned. The cars were taken home to their "stables," and although a few whizzed about the streets long into the night, the evening was quiet and peaceful compared with the noise and excitement of the day.

THE AUTOMOBILE BALL

The ball on Monday night in the Kursaal was a brilliant affair. The Kursaal assuredly never looked more charming than with its delicate festoons and sprays of smilax, the delightful fresh green of which was set off by dainty pink blossoms, real foliage and flowers being employed. The effect beneath the softened light of the tiny coloured lamps was very pleasing. Pink hydrangeas in baskets were placed within the woodwork of the arches, and large palms and geraniums in pots decorated the lounge between the ball-room and the deck. The decorations were in the hands of Messrs. Goodyear, of Bond-street, who are to be congratulated on the result of their efforts. The floor had been admirably prepared by Messrs. Cunningham, Barfett, and Co., a special dancing drugget giving a capital surface. The decoration of the reception department and lounge was also in the hands of this firm; the Oriental rugs and carpets presented a luxurious appearance. The decoration of the stage (with a tropical scene in the background) was universally admired. The front was a mass of the choicest Indian azaleas, geraniums, fuchsias, ferns, and foliage, set off with lofty palms. In front, upon a glass-covered stand, were displayed the dress prizes; the arch above was lighted with red and white lights alternately. A space in front of the stage was carpeted, and a row of chairs faced the ball-room. Great praise for the general arrangements of the room is due to Messrs. R. Welch, Loates, Osborne, and other attendants, who worked hard to ensure that the details should be thoroughly carried out.

The De La Warr Orchestra, conducted by Mr J. M. Glover, rendered selections of dance music, which were much enjoyed.

THE PROGRAMME

March........ "The Invincible Eagle."	Barn......... "Honeysuckle and Bee."
Valse............... "The New Century."	Lancers...................... "Casino Girl."
Polka.......... "Retour des Champs."	Valse.................... "Cambrolieurs."
Valse................... "Amorettentanz."	CakeWalk......... "Whistling Rufus."
Barn Dance................ "Dolly Gray."	Valse............................ "La Gitana."
Lancers........................... "San Toy."	Lancers...................... "Kitty Grey."
Valse................ "Tresor d'Amour."	Polka .... "See Me Dance."
Barn Dance.......... "The Ballet Girl."	Valse.................................. "Bleue."
Lancers.... "The Popular Number."	Barn Dance............. "Sunny South."
Valse..................... "Liebestraume."	Lancers.......... "The Silver Slipper."
Valse.................. "Donau Wellen."	Valse................... "Wiener Burger."
	Valse.............. "Old Times Coach."

Dancing commenced about 10.30, by which time a good number were present. A large crowd outside watched the arrival of the dancers, whose varied costumes imparted great animation to the scene inside. The Orchestra was playing its best. By the time the third item on the programme — the polka, "Retour des champs" — had been reached, shortly before eleven o'clock, the ball-room was full. The barn dance, "Dolly Gray," was very popular. Conversation was brisk in the intervals between the dances.

The supper (laid at twelve o'clock) was supplied by the Sackville Hotel in very recherche style. The following is the menu.

MENU

Souper de Bal   19th May, 1902.
Consomme Reche en Tasse.

—

Œufs Tosca. — Filets de Sole Richelieu. — Aspic de Crevettes.

—

Galantine de Volaille. — Filet de Bœuf Renaissance. — Mousse de Jambon a la Neva.
Langue Ecarlate. — Sandwiches Assorties.

—

Patisserie Varies.

—

Granite au Cafe. — Glace Praline.

—

Petits Fours Sackville.

The next Bexhill event was not held again until two years later over the August Bank Holiday of 1904. A Mr William Mayner who had objected to the event, sought and won an injuction in the Chancery division of the High Court against the Earl De La Warr using the Marine Road for racing. As a consequence the 1903 event could not be held at Bexhill so the ACGBI, who had leased the use of the Bexhill track for a number of years, decided that year to use the Duke of Portland's Welbeck Estate with his permission.

Alterations to the track excluding the use of the Marine Road meant that Bexhill could once again stage its event in 1904 and thereafter.

Memories of both the 1904 and 1902 events were printed in the Saturday June 19th 1954 souvenir edition of the *Bexhill-on-Sea Observer* on the day that Bexhill celebrated its Jubilee. The following text is taken in part from that 1954 edition.

The first motor racing in Britain

Jubilee of Bexhill's famous 1904 'Petrol Derby' recalls

MEMORIES OF MOTOR RACING 50 YEARS AGO

Fifty years ago Bexhill was the centre of British motor racing. On Whit-Monday, 1902, the town staged "the first serious contest ever held in England."

On August Bank Holiday, 1904, famous motorists came from France and all over Britain to compete in a three-day "Petrol Derby."

This afternoon, as cars that are legendary names in motoring history, speed along East Parade, Bexhill will re-live these glories of an enterprising past.

IDEA BORN TWO YEARS AGO

Today's occasion is the S. F. Edge Trophy Meeting or Jubilee Speed Trials, organised by the Veteran Car Club of Great Britain, to commemorate the 1904 event. The idea of a jubilee rally and trials was put forward two years ago by Mrs Edge, a vice-president of the V.C.C., and widow of Mr S. F. Edge, the brilliant pioneer motorist.

Mrs Edge, who lives at 10, Jameson-road, Bexhill, has donated the trophy awarded to her husband as the most successful competitor in the 1904 races, to the club and she will present it personally to this year's winner.

Officials expect that more than 10,000 spectators will watch this afternoon's trials, which will be photographed by television, Gaumont-British and Pathé newsreel cameras.

As Mr Edge won the principal trophy in 1904 with a Napier car it is fitting that the marque Napier should be represented this year by two entries, including the great 60 h.p. model of 1907 entered by Mr R. L. Green and Mr L. Willis, for this played a great part in the success of the firm during the time that Mr Edge led its commercial activities. The Napier will compete with such fast cars as Mr W. A. L. Cook's 1908 45 h.p. Mercedes and the 1913 80/90 h.p. model entered by Mr A. W. F. Smith.

Busy scene outside the Sackville Hotel on the morning of the start of the 1904 Bexhill event.

An entry of special interest to Bexhill is that of 80-year-old Mr Frederick Stanley Bennett, President of the Veteran Car Club, who visited Bexhill in September last with his "Old Dutch" —the name he has given to his 1903 single-cylinder Cadillac—when he was taking part in a 1,000-mile reliability trial.

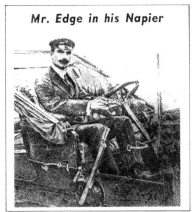

Mr. Edge in his Napier

Mr S. F. Edge pictured in his Napier in 1907. This was the year he celebrated the opening of the famous Brooklands track (17 June) with his famous solo record attempt driving for 24 hours non-stop (28-29 June) in his 60 hp Napier.

Not so well known is that earlier he had taken another record: Edge had broken Serpollet's long-standing 1902 Bexhill record run, when he registered a speed of 73.4 mph in his Napier along the Bexhill sea-front track.

Bexhill still has strong links with its motoring past, first of all due to Mrs S. F. Edge, on whose initiative the Veteran Car Club decided to organise the commemorative rally and trials being held today. Mrs Edge told the *Observer*: "I had the idea of a jubilee commemoration event at Bexhill two years ago when I was attending a club rally. Everyone seemed so enthusiastic, and so I

50

held them to it. There is no reason why the races should not be a great success. We have had every co-operation from the Bexhill Corporation, and I think the club might well come back to Bexhill in future years."

Napier Triumph

The premier award of the day, the S. F. Edge 1904 Bexhill Trophy, has been given by Mrs Edge to the club as a perpetual challenge trophy for their annual speed event. The late Mr Edge was presented with the 90-ounce trophy for winning Class G (large cars priced between £750 and £1,000) at the 1904 meeting. Records show that in the final in his 20 h.p. Napier he beat two high-powered Daimlers, the 26 h.p. model driven by Mr W. Stratton and the 28 h.p. driven by Mr Percy Martin. Before that he had beaten some of the finest Continental makes, including the 60 h.p. Mercedes. Mrs Edge was a young girl on holiday in Bexhill with her grandparents in 1904 and watched the races, little knowing that one of the competitors was her future husband.

The 'Edge' Trophy was the premier award at the 1904 Bexhill meeting. The original inscription read: First prize, Bexhill, 1904, won by S. F. Edge, Class G. A new inscription reads: Presented by Mrs S. F. Edge at Bexhill, 1954, as a perpetual challenge trophy for the annual speed event of the Veteran Car Club of Great Britain in memory of the late S. F. Edge and his 25 years of racing.

In his 25 years of racing Mr Edge performed many outstanding feats. Mrs Edge recalled a few. . .

1902 when he brought the Gordon-Bennett trophy awarded for

Europe's most gruelling motor test, to England for the first and only time. . .

1907 the year the Brooklands track was opened, and he drove continuously for 24 hours, a record which stood for 15 years. . .

1923 when at Brooklands he competed for the last time, winning a double 12-hour race.

Mr Edge was one of the original members and a vice-president of the Veteran Car Club. After his death Mrs Edge was invited to become a vice-president, a position she holds today.

Family Record

Then there is Mr H. J. Mulliner, of Bayworth, Terminus-avenue, Bexhill, who is among the most distinguished of the select band of pioneers. 84, Mr Mulliner has been in motoring since its 'Red Flag' days, and for his work in the developments of the automobile he was made an honorary life member of the V.C.C. in 1948. It reads like a citation, and indeed it is, for the Mulliner family's tradition and their services to transport, go back over five centuries.

In the 15th century Mr Mulliner's ancestors kept pack horses; in the 17th century they built coaches, and at the turn of the last century they helped to speed the mechanical evolution on its way by directing their attention to developing the 'horseless carriage.' They understood the requirements of the age and made provision with flourishing success.

A founder-member and honorary life member of the Royal Automobile Club, Mr Mulliner branched out in the family tradition, and set up as a motor carriage builder in Brook-street, London, in 1896. Hard work and ability brought their reward; he had orders from the late Queen Mary when she was Princess of Wales, Indian rajahs and a 'sprinkling of Debrett.' From those beginnings grew his firm of H. J. Mulliner and Co. Ltd., from which he severed connection when he retired in 1910.

In 1896 he recalls a grey November day when he and Mr Charles Rolls, of Rolls-Royce fame, drove round Grosvenor-square, led by a man with the obligatory red flag. The next day — November 14 — he watched the start of the historic run to

Brighton to celebrate the legalising of the motor on British roads, and the following year he himself took part in the run.

He himself drove for 46 years until 1941 when he got rid of his car. Today he will be watching from the grandstand at Galley Hill.

NEWSPAPER'S ENTHUSIASM OVER EARLY MEETING

Although today's Veteran Car Club rally commemorates the jubilee of the celebrated races of 1904, that was not the first occasion on which Bexhill had won the limelight by such enterprising demonstrations. Two years earlier *Motoring Illustrated* had reported:–

The great Bexhill motor races and speed trials were carried out on Whit-Monday under circumstances that completely demonstrated that the horseless carriage has become a permanent institution, and that it is not, as a few fossils have been professing, a mere temporary importation from France.

'Patron Saint'

The importance of the event may be judged from the coverage given to it by the magazine — seven pages of reports, good quality photographs and pointed comments, such as this one, which is of special interest in the light of recent attempts to establish a new motor racing track:–

About 200 of the best motor cars in England braved the raw, chilly days of mid-May — 'Wet Monday' someone called it — to appear at Bexhill, the watering place which has put itself in the front line of progress through its racecourse, established by the enterprise and exertions of the Earl De La Warr.

The Earl is the patron saint of Bexhill. He made a thriving town where a few years ago only daisies flourished. He created a motor track as if by magic. It is on his own private property, and it one of the few places in England where the speeding automobilist is absolutely sure of being safe from the raids of antediluvian policemen.

'Petrol Derby'

Not only was the meet the biggest ever held by the Automobile

Club, but it was by all odds the most important. It marked the completion of a kilometre race track for the holding of Petrol Derbies. This is the first in England dedicated to the motorist. Who can say the races of the future will not be wholly mechanical, or that the petted jockey will not be obsolete while bookmakers and betters lay their money for and against the motor car?

Evidently "the first serious contest ever held in England" was not regarded with a kindly eye by the law, for the report comments scathingly:–

The Surrey magistrates and police scented the meet from afar, and, putting their heads together — it was whispered that a hollow ring was heard as they did this — devised the usual plots to capture and fine motorists. The police hid in hedges, under the encouragement of the magistrates, and arranged signal systems for proving that cars were travelling more than 12 miles an hour. Over their cigars competitors told of police persecution in Uckfield, though which they ran the gauntlet; of horsemen with untrained hacks, which proved a nuisance. One had collided with a cow, and others had had adventures equally heroic.

3-Day Meeting

After the success of the 1902 event an ambitious programme was drawn up for the three-day meeting in 1904. For a whole week the town, gay with decorations and illuminations, offered attractive entertainment for the competitors and the thousands of people who came into Bexhill to watch the racing.

A "procession of cars" or Concours d'Elegance led the series of events; there was a battle of flowers, gymkhana and a Bal Masque, all of which were extremely successful, "and the incidental pleasures of the Park fetes, and the musical and theatrical performances at the Kursaal."

London newspaper correspondents attended the race meeting and gave long and eulogistic notices, while the *Bexhill Observer* devoted four of its 16 pages to reports and comments on every aspect, and also published a four-page photographic "automobile supplement," handsomely printed on art paper.

Smiling Police

The *Daily Telegraph*'s special correspondent effused:–

At sunny Bexhill this morning King petrol began a glorious, if brief and somewhat highly-scented, reign. In Bexhill for the moment, to vary Kipling's line, "there ain't no legal limit, and a car can go a burst." The roads have all been Westrumited, and over them cars career at considerably more than the lawful 20 m.p.h., what time the police smile benignly and the inhabitants look on with keen and friendly interest. For the auspices of the Automobile Club, a three-days Motor carnival is being held, the hotels are full of the devotees of the petrol habit, and thousands of sightseers have lined the track to watch today's events.

Marine-parade is gay with bunting, and most of the houses are decorated. Automobilists in festive garb – a very different raiment from that worn for serious travelling – swarm about the Sackville Hotel.

New Era Dawned

In high-flown prose a correspondent of the *Daily Chronicle* – now amalgamated in the *News Chronicle* – wrote an appreciation:–

Bexhill is the latest thing in watering places, a modern creation, smart, stylish and ambitious. It possesses a Continental flavour and is a miniature Ostend without the Casino. It has a Kursaal with a difference, and yet a dozen years ago it was a mere village overlooking Pevensey Bay. It offered no temptation to those who desired recreation by the sea, and very few strangers ever sought rest between its narrow boundaries. . .

Then suddenly a new era dawned for Bexhill. It conceived new ambitions and set itself to earn the approval of those who had hitherto given their patronage to other watering places. Lord De La Warr, chief landlord of the district and lord of the manor, took an active part in the movements, and with astounding rapidity the simple village grew into a large and fashionable watering-place.

It was with the growth of the automobile that Bexhill came to the front. While the gods in the car were still harried by a pertinacious constabulary and frowned upon by unsympathetic laws, Bexhill offered them hospitality and accommodation.

This marvellous photo of the wreckage of a 24 hp Napier appears in the book Brands to Bexhill.
Little is known other than the date 17th August 1907. It also featured in the book Motor Mania
with a silly caption suggesting nothing this 'exciting' had happened at Bexhill for ages. It is clear
that Bexhill was still attracting prominent racers even with Brooklands operational. Having studied
the picture closely I feel sure the person on the right with the concerned expression is Cecil Edge,
cousin of S. F. Edge. Alan Vessey, Hon. Sec. of Napier Power Heritage says he agrees with me.

Had Cecil Edge, who raced several cars five years earlier at the historic 1902 event, been at the wheel of this Napier and in what event, if any, was it partaking? What is the real story behind this intriguing picture? Accidents on the Bexhill track had been conspicuous by their almost total absence. The 24th May 1902 Bexhill Chronicle *stated: The Automobile Club are more than satisfied with Bexhill's track. It would be surprising if it were not made the venue of the greatest motor contests of the future.*

This picture shows some of the competitors cars which competed in the 1904 Bexhill rally housed in the Down Drill Hall. In the background is motor engineer Mr Louis Russell seated on the Vulcan car in which he competed. He founded Russells in 1896 on the same London Road site in Bexhill that it occupies today. The story goes that Louis Russell met the other famous Louis (Renault) at the Bexhill Races and together formed an alliance which remains as the longest-standing Renault agency in the UK, now run by his grandson John Russell.

A Race underway in 1904 along the Bexhill course.

'Digging' into the past to unearth more about the Bexhill Whitsun event continues unabated. The following is an edited version of a feature by Cliff Hopkins in the May 1997 Bexhill 100 programme courtesy of D C Graphics and Brian Hazell.

The Stone and the Cup

Bexhill Town Council were sponsors of one of the events at the Bexhill Races in 1902. They commissioned a solid silver trophy, the Bexhill 30 Guineas Cup, to be awarded to the car having the best appearance (similar to a Concours de Elegance today).

The question of what happened to this particular cup and its whereabouts remained unanswered until a chance meeting.

The Stone

A stroll along Bexhill's promenade will lead you to a stone which commemorates the speed trials of 1902, the birthplace of British motor racing. A Bexhill newcomer, Ian Bush, noticed this stone while peering down from the window of his sea-front flat, which he was in the process of buying. On a visit to his estate agent Ian enquired about the stone asking why was it was placed there? As his agent Brian Hazell was a director and one of the founders of the Bexhill 100 (and like all good estate agents, never at a loss for words), he related the history of the races to Ian.

Having listened to Brian's narrative, Ian recalled that his father had told tales of a distant relative, a pioneer motorist and world billiards champion. Could there be a connection? A few days later Ian returned to Brian's office armed with information he had received from Madame Joyce Birchmeier-Peall (now living in Switzerland), granddaughter of William J Peall. The archives revealed that W J Peall had taken part at the inaugural races and it was he who had won the Bexhill 30 Guineas Cup (*see p. 45*).

William John Peall was born on the 31st December 1854 in the Parish of St Pancras, London. By the age of twelve he had learned the game of billiards and he soon became a talented amateur. Fourteen years later he took part in a professional tournament, although receiving no prize money, he was adjudged by a section of the press to be a professional. He was not pleased, because in his own words, as an amateur he was 'somebody', but had a big chance of being 'nobody' among the great professionals. However, he accepted the position without grousing, a characteristic which marked his whole career.

W J Peall set to his task, and energetically practised the spot stroke, and he soon became master. At a Command performance at Windsor Castle, King Edward expressed a wish to see him make a break of 500 'off the spot.' He did it at the first try, although once or twice the balls ran awkwardly.

In 1890 Peall held the record for the highest break of 3,304 points, three days before his opponent got to the table. It took 55 years before his record was finally broken by Walter Lindrum.

By now William Peall was a household name and in spite of being just 5 ft 1 in tall his professional career flourished. He was an astute man and invested his winnings with the purchase of an inn at the bottom of Brixton Hill in London where, in between contests, he would stage exhibition matches. In 1892 he became the English Billiards Champion before becoming World Billiards Champion a few years later.

William J Peall pictured at the wheel of one of his cars. On this occasion his 8 hp Panhard

Early in 1898, at the age of 43, he was bitten by the motoring bug. With irrepressible enthusiasm he purchased his first car, an 8 hp Mors Dogcart, with air-cooled engine, belt drive and surface carburettor. It was a calamity, rarely venturing out without needing a tow home at the rear of a horse, all to the accompaniment of jeers from the public. When asked about the attitude of the public in those days to motorists, he replied: 'Very hostile. In the early days if you met a restive horse you had to stop. Sometimes a driver would try to get his horse used to the motor but more often they were antagonistic. Horse drivers had a nasty trick of pretending to flick the horse with their whip, only to flick your ear, which was very painful.'

Buying a car in those days often consisted of going to a motor exhibition, where cars would be arranged round the sides of the arena. You took it for granted having bought the car that it would go up hills and that the brakes would hold it going down — indeed, going downhill could be it perilous adventure. The brake was a pad fitted to a back wheel, like the brake on a cart. If the back brake was used too much it could strip the tread from the tyres, or even cause the wooden blocks to catch fire.

This picture was taken outside one of the first purpose-built garages at W J Peall's home in Brixton.
Fuel was stored in a pit inside the garage in 2 gallon containers which were delivered by either Shell or Pratts.

The caption to the picture reads: Ernest (Peall?), W J Peall, Mabel (wife?) and Gordon (son, out of picture shot?)

It was at such a show in Islington, London that he bought his second car, a 6 hp Daimler — far more reliable than the Mors. At this time one of his sons, Gordon, was introduced to motoring and in 1901 he took part in a non-stop run form London to Southsea. This was such an achievement that he was awarded a special diploma from the Automobile Club of Great Britain and Ireland (ACGBI). In 1903 at the age of 21, Gordon became involved in the development of the motor industry, working with Messrs Brotherhood Crocker Motors Ltd who built their first car in West

Norwood, South London. Unreliability caused the company to cease building cars. Gordon later joined the Du Cros organisation selling the 'Gladiator'. Encouraged by his father he then started his own business in 1909 until 1916. During the Great War he was building aero engines at Weybridge — the 'Clerget' as used in great numbers by the Royal Flying Corps.

Peall's love of the automobile occasionally got him into trouble. Once when 'speeding' down Brixton Hill, unfortunately for him the police had set up a speed trap. The police gave chase... on foot (speed limit was 12 mph). Newspaper headlines read: 'Billy Peall pursued by Peelers.' A cartoon in *Punch* showed the Peelers puffing and blowing as they chased his car down Brixton Hill.

W. J. Peall at the wheel of his superb 12 hp Daimler – the body designed and built to his own specification by Mulliner – in which he won the Bexhill 30 Guineas Cup *at the 1902 Bexhill Races. He lost out on the* House of Commons Cup *as he insisted on driving whilst wearing his famous felt hat. Judges docked him points for his unorthodox attire!*

The Cup

What happened to W J Peall and the Bexhill Cup? The old billiard champion eventually retired from professional play and moved from Brixton to Hove on the Sussex coast, when at 94 years of age he decided to confine his motoring to private roads. He was Britain's oldest motorist. His last car was a 1947 Vauxhall Fourteen, successor to a long series of early Daimlers, Panhards, Gladiators, Austins and Buicks. Sadly this great sportsman and pioneer motorist died in 1952 at the age of 98.

But what of the cup? ... Regrettably it is no longer with us. In 1926 the depression caused many people to consolidate their future by selling off the family silver. William Peall was no exception and sold most of his trophies, cutlery and so on, and invested in property. The cup became a molten blob. However, one trophy did remain: the World Professional Billiards Trophy, a magnificent gilt urn of classic design, ornamented with delicate silver filigree and laurel leaves.

In 1952, acting on Peall's wishes his family generously donated the magnificent trophy to the Royal Automobile Club, where it still is today and known as the Peall Cup. Each year since 1953 (when it went to the British rally driver Ian Appleyard) this trophy has been awarded to the winner of the RAC Rally. Many famous drivers of different nationalities have held the trophy. The present holder, winner of the 1996 RAC Rally, is Colin McRae.

The late W. J. Peall, Master of the spot stroke, World Billiards Champion.
This magnificent trophy is now awarded each year to the winner of the RAC Rally.

Over page: What might have been. In 1906 the Earl de la Warr had plans drawn up for a new and ambitious National Motor Course at nearby Cooden, with an 8 mile circuit and full facilities for motor racing. Brooklands stole the thunder from the Earl – the rest is history.

63

The first motor racing in Britain

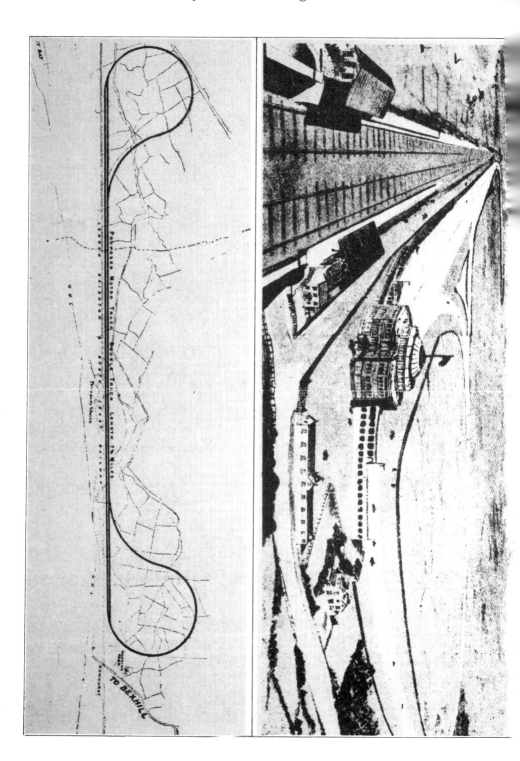